Love

- ➤ He who dares not grasp the thorn should never crave the rose.

- ➤ I was never meant for surface level. I was always meant for intensity, depth and intimacy. That's where my heart lies.

- ➤ She wants to be loved unconditionally for an eternity.

- ➤ Running from parts of yourself that you're unwilling to change to be worthy of her is cowardice. True love will do whatever it takes without making excuses.

- ➤ Someone who cares about the reason behind my quiet moments, who wants to understand the storms inside me rather than judge the calm I show on the outside. A connection where silence isn't seen as something wrong but as a safe place where my thoughts can breathe without fear of anger or misunderstanding.

➤ Intimacy is being understood. Going to bookstores together. Knowing glances. Being your weird self around them. Someone who doesn't make you feel dumb for not knowing about certain things. Sharing childhood memories. Sharing your past. Someone who patiently listens to even the most mundane stuff. I believe in you. Finding someone who doesn't mind staying home on weekends. Finishing each other's sentences. I got your favourite snack. Feeling at home within their arms. Reading their zodiac sign along with yours. When you feel deeply seen and heard by them. This song reminds me of you. Being each other's go to person. Quality time. Being vulnerable with each other. Admitting your fears. Being appreciated for all the tiny details that make up who you are.

➤ I'm the warrior who needs a place to rest between my battles so be my home and hero.

D'DECLARATIONS

Untangled Soul

of a

Shattered Romantic

GNANAMBHIKAIY GANAPATHI

INDIA · SINGAPORE · MALAYSIA

ISBN 979-8-89744-699-5

➤ She takes care of everything and everyone but sometimes she wants to be taken care of too. Every once in a while, the tiredness overtakes her and she is overcome with a weary loneliness and the simple need to be taken care of.

➤ What did you lose to that makes you chase love so much?

➤ To fall so deeply in love with someone and investing my life into theirs only to discover that they do not feel the same way. To me, that is how you die while still breathing and you can never recover from that no matter how hard you try. That's what I'm afraid of.

➤ Someone asked me "What's one dream you gave up on?"

➤ I answered "Being loved".

➤ The thing about people who haven't been loved much. They think about every kind gesture, a slightest touch of fingers, kind smiles, random acts of love, intimacy in every small thing done. They find that love wherever they can cause it was never given to them freely.

➤ You know you really love someone when you don't hate them for breaking your heart.

➤ Don't break up. Fix the problem. Start the romance again. Go on dates again. Work on winning each other over again. This is why there are so many failed relationships. If you love each other and are best friends, then breaking up is not the answer.

➤ I think once the heart is broken, nothing will ever be the same again. Yes, one can heal but it's never the same. You become a lot stronger. You learn to find yourself & who you are. You grow up, you mature & you become bolder. It's all a learning process. Yes, it is all an experience. But you'll never be the person you were before. As much as you try, it will never be the same.

➤ Sometimes, every so often, I wonder, every moment of our lives pass by our eyes as fast as the speed of light. Loved ones lost & loved ones gained & loved ones who still remain the same. Lost love, unrequited love, broken hearts. As much dismay as it may have caused, it's those lessons that make us who we are today.

➤ Anyone can say that they love you but not everyone can choose you when things around you get so difficult. The reality of love is to always choose that person over anything.

➤ When you love someone, you love all of them. You gotta love everything about them. Not just the good things but the bad things too. The things that you find lovable & the things that you don't find lovable.

➤ Give her two red roses, each with a note. The first one says "For the woman I love" and the second "for my best friend".

➤ It is true that I've had heartache & tragedy in my life. These are things none of us avoids. Suffering is the price of being alive.

➤ Meeting you was fate, becoming your friend was a choice but falling in love with you I had no control over.

➤ Tears are words the heart can't express.

➢ The intimacy of eye contact. Smirks across a crowded room. Raised eyebrows. Knowing glances. Witty banter. The sides of legs accidentally touching in the backseat. Dancing in front of strangers. Playful teasing. Comfortable silences. Quiet time. Falling asleep together. The little things. The inside jokes. Appreciation. Mutual trust. Heart to heart conversations. Sharing books with your scribbles. "I've never told another person that before." First hugs. A kiss you crave for. "I heard this song and thought of you." "I'm so sorry." A sense of safety. Just knowing someone is here to stay, even though you have no real evidence for thinking so. Believing they will anyway.

➢ It's hard to wait around for something you know might never happen but it's even harder to give up when it's everything you want.

➢ When the whole world turned its back on you, she stayed even when her own world was falling apart. She was the girl who begged in silence for your attention while you were too busy noticing others. She was the girl who saw the best in you even when you showed her the worst. In the end, after giving everything she had, she left quietly not because she stopped loving you but because she realized you never truly loved her back.

➤ Most men lose their woman to the slow death of their own edge and the absence of the fire she once saw in his eyes. Most women do not fantasize about other men, they wake up fantasizing about the man you used to be. Feeling the way they once did with you. When you made her feel alive, feminine, seen, desired and safe. When you were a force. She drifted away not because she found something better but because you abandoned yourself.

➤ When you're in love & you get hurt, it's like a cut. The pain heals with time but the scars will never fade.

➤ We come to love not by finding a perfect person but by learning to see an imperfect person perfectly.

➤ A woman's head is always influenced by her heart but a man's heart is always influenced by his head.

- ➤ Once you have taken a rose from its vine, you cannot put it back. Just like once you have taken love from her soul, you cannot put it back together.

- ➤ When she lets you in, it's not because she needs you. She stopped needing people a long time ago. It's because she genuinely wants you. That's love right there.

- ➤ No matter what has happened in the past, no matter how many stupid things you've done or how many bad decisions you've made, you're still worthy of absolution. Still worthy of hope, encouragement, and compassion. Most importantly, you're worthy of being loved and being seen as you are now, not who you used to be. Forgive yourself and forget the memories that no longer serve you. Accept grace. Dare to acknowledge that you have learnt from your mistakes.

- ➤ I pass lovers on the street couples holding hands, strolling in harmony, looking like they belong together and think to myself : I hope he is good to her, I hope he keeps her safe, I hope she feels his love from her head right down to her toes. I hope she gets everything that I don't.

➤ Rarity is having enough emotional and mental patience and maturity to work through the obstacles. To communicate and to lose the ego because you value the connection more than your pride. You have the to leave your ego at the door in love. It's a must.

➤ Because I finally realized I can't force you to choose me, no matter how badly I want you to. Because I finally realized I can't make you love me the way I love you, even though all I crave is your affection and desire. Because I finally realized that I met you when I wasn't looking for you but I lost you when I loved you the most.

➤ Even in a thousand lifetimes, I would face the same trials, endure the same heartbreaks, and feel the same losses, if it meant I'd find my way back to you.

➤ For him, it was just a mistake. For her, it became a lifetime of trauma, insecurities, trust issues, and the haunting feeling of being unworthy of love. A scar that even time cannot erase.

➤ Talk to date. Date to marry. Marry to grow old together. The only way it should be.

➤ Love her extra on her bad days. She'll get too emotional, too clingy, and she might get angry at small things. Instead of getting mad at her, be extra patient with her. Those are the days she needs your love and patience the most.

➤ If you think she didn't care, you probably didn't see her at 2am crying her heart out. Trying to piece together where she went wrong, why you changed so much all while holding herself back from falling apart. The pain of being hurt from the person who once made her feel whole. That heartbreak is like nothing else.

➤ What if staying is all she ever needed from you? Will you leave her wondering if she was never enough or will you finally show her that she is?

➤ She never got the things she liked. She was always the one who observes, but never the observed. She was always the one who loves but was never loved. She craves love, yet she never got that.

➤ You cannot immediately unlove what you loved unless you never loved it anyway.

➤ Always a fool in love, never the loved. Always the artist, never the muse. Always an option, never the chosen one. Always the listener, never the talker. Always lost, never found. Always the poet, never the verse. Always the heart, never the beat. Always the soul, never the home.

➤ A toast to me, always the bridesmaid never the bride.

➤ You deserve someone who can see your messy hair, pale lips, pimples, eyebags, unattractive clothes or in short, see the worst in you but still find you beautiful.

➤ One day, you'll realize that she was the girl that stayed up with you, she was the girl who spent every day talking to you, she was the girl who made sure you were okay, she was the girl who spent every day waiting to talk to you, she was the girl who unfriended every guy for you, she was the girl who stayed even after you said mean things to her, she was the girl who loved you even after you pushed her away many times and she was the girl who loved you more than she loved herself. She was the girl who would put you before yourself. She was the girl who showed you what real love looks like.

➤ A man doesn't run from brokenness. He understands it, respects it and helps carry the weight.

➤ Emotional distance doesn't stem from the occasional argument, it grows when you're made to feel invisible, when your needs aren't met and when your feelings are invalidated. When your needs are constantly dismissed and neglected, the connection slowly fades and an emptiness begins to grow. It's the absence of care, acknowledgement and understanding that deepens the divide leaving you feeling your feelings and needs don't matter which leads to emotional isolation in what should be a partnership.

➢ Instead of walking away, make it work. Love is hard.

➢ I sat with my anger and asked why it kept showing up. It said because you've been hurt & no one listened. I sat with my sadness and asked why it never left. It said because I'm the love & care you never received. I sat with my fear and asked why it controlled me. It said because there is a part of you that's still waiting to feel safe. Then I realized these feelings weren't my enemies. They were my wounds asking to be seen.

➢ Two people can have different backgrounds, interests or ways of thinking, but love grows when they're willing to adjust, compromise and find a middle ground. It's not about finding someone who fits perfectly into your life but someone who's willing to build a life together. Love is more about becoming the one who chooses to stay, to listen and to work through hard times.

➢ When you genuinely love a person, you work on those negative traits and learn to communicate, you listen to each other's feelings, thoughts and emotions.

➤ Things she loves but won't ask for: flowers, reassurance, random calls, random dates, random lunch at work sent to her, love letters, forehead kisses, always being reminded that she's loved, random gifts, quality time, shopping with her, long hugs, deep conversations, random thoughtful texts, holding hands and on her period, something she loves like chocolates or sweets.

➤ Devotion, the purest form of love & loyalty. Seeing the good in you & the potential that you have, not the hurtful things you said and did. Just remember that the next time you call her crazy or dramatic because she never deserved that.

➤ She's as soft as a flower yet strong as the storm.

➤ The storms in my head ruined the garden that my soul holds.

➤ Old souls love differently. They would notice your every tiny detail & cherish every moment with you. Their actions would scream their heart out. They would spoil you with your favourite stuff & enjoy even the mundane things. From holding hands to tight hugs to cuddling to little kisses, they would simply adore you. They adore all the little moments. They would be afraid to show you their vulnerable side but still would never give up on you. They would love to love you for who you are.

➤ You lost interest in me and I lost interest on everything. You lost only me and I lost almost everything. When I was nothing to you, you were my whole world. I was a disturbance to you and you were the only thing I wanted. You didn't like me and your name was the only one I chanted. After reading her words, he realized what she had been through. He said "I never lost interest, I just never knew how to love you the way you deserved. But if there's still a chance, I'm ready to learn with you for as long as it takes".

➤ Realizing that when you're in a relationship with someone who genuinely wants to grow with you, they will always bring up problems that doesn't sit right with them to your attention. It isn't a personal attack. It's a healthy sign that they value the relationship and want to make it work. All they are doing is bringing it to your attention to avoid the same mistake so the relationship doesn't go down the drain.

➤ Always choose to care. Choose to stay messy hearted in a world that may not always be kind to you. Choose to do whatever you have to do to make it tomorrow. Choose to get up in the morning when you do not want to, choose to face what is scarred within you. Work on every single day to be gentle and soft with yourself even when you have been given every reason to harden. Choose to feel everything intensely and do not apologize for your power, your hope or the way you slam yourself into the human beings you meet. Choose to shout your love from rooftops, choose to share your heart with the world. Choose to fight to be better, to heal even when it hurts, to believe with everything you hold within yourself that you have purpose here.

➤ I don't regret a single ounce of love I gave. Their choices don't define me. What matters is that I stayed true to myself and to the love I was willing to give. I gave loyalty and kindness because I believe in it. That's who I am and I never lost sight of who I am.

➤ I still feel the bittersweetness when I see others around me getting engaged and married. I won't lie, when I watch others step into a new season of life, hand in hand with someone they love, having weathered the storms together, I can't help but feel a mixture of awe, joy, excitement, and a bit of sadness. The sadness isn't directed at them, but reflects my own place in life. At one point, I truly thought that would be me, and now, I look back and chuckle at the thought, because life has shown me how far from that I am. I do long to love and be loved by someone beside me. I always have and somewhere deep inside, that longing still waits. Not in a desperate way but with hope. I hope for a love that makes me feel like a child experiencing Disney World for the first time, where dreams really do come true.

Can dreams still come true, even when they feel so far away?

➤ I thought I wasn't ready for her but I wish I would've been patient. She was there for me and ready to grow with me no matter what but I didn't realize until it was too late. Don't waste time thinking you need more time. Time doesn't wait.

➤ I never stopped loving you. I stopped believing in you. I stopped holding onto the hope you'd change. I stopped letting myself feel small while I gave everything you wouldn't even think of giving back. I stopped because I realized I couldn't keep letting the same person hurt me the same way over and over. I would've lost every part of myself just trying ti be enough for you.

➤ It hurts her deeply because deep down she knows you're a good person with so much love to offer but when you act in ways that are completely different, she starts second-guessing everything. Is she seeing the real you or just the version she hopes for? The disconnect between who you truly are and who you show her is breaking her heart.

➤ To the one I love, I will wake you up with soft kisses every morning. I will try my best not to get irritated when you tease me. I will let you burn the pancakes and eat them with a smile on my face. I won't push you away when I'm down. I will let you hug me until I feel better. I will be crazy and loud with you. I will go on as many walks with you as you want, even if the park looks like something out of a horror movie. I will kiss your cheeks, your eyes and the big grin on your face. I will hear your side of the story even if I'm angry. I will let you decide where we go for dinner. I won't say anything when you wear your favourite shirt that I really don't like. I will hold your hand when you need it the most. I will be there for you. I will kiss you every time you feel alone. I will love you always unconditionally.

➤ How do you love so deep and so hard when you have never been loved the same in return? You see, I never want anyone to ever feel alone as me.

➤ People are never happy with what they have. People easily get tempted and commit. People easily get bored. Instead of putting efforts to sort it out, people assume and give up. We need to train our minds not to get tempted easily. To focus on inner beauty. To be grateful. To focus on our commitments and our values for our partner.

➤ I noticed everything:

➤ I noticed when you weren't excited about my presence anymore, I noticed when you started getting more distant, I noticed when talking to me felt like a chore to you, I noticed when you stopped putting in effort for us, I noticed you got ruder, I noticed you stopped asking to do things together, I noticed everything about us.

➤ When you let your partner sleep with a heavy heart, you're ignoring their pain. Real love isn't about waiting for things to settle on their own. It's about acknowledging that their feelings matter. Letting them carry that pain into the night doesn't make it disappear it creates more distance. You don't need all the answers but you can't let silence speak for you. It's not about fixing everything, it's about being present together.

➤ Effort. Consistency. Assurance. Show me you care. That you really want me. I'm tired of doubting.

➤ We started to argue more often and I lost hope thinking we might divorce. I reminded myself I had the most beautiful woman on earth. I showered her with flowers, kisses and compliments. I gave her gifts, lived for her and spoke about her with pride. She started to bloom in ways I'd never seen before. A woman is a reflection of the man who loves her. When a man loves her deeply, she becomes everything he ever dreamed of. Actions speak louder than words.

➤ Never again will I be the low maintenance girlfriend, that is not an image I want to keep up just so a man feels like he can do the bare minimum and still have me around. I like flowers I don't have to ask for, I like dates that I don't have to plan. I like reassurance, love letters, notes, long texts, and updates I don't have to ask for. I like my partner cooking for me, I like photos of us on your social media accounts, I like acts of service and small suprises. And I'm tired of pretending I don't.

➤ Your love made me a beggar, a beggar who begs for your replies, a beggar who begs for your time, a beggar who begs for your smile, a beggar who begs for your love. I beg for the way you used to look at me, for the warmth that once burned in your eyes, for the hands that once held me close, for the lips that once whispered stay close. You have made me a beggar and yet, I beg again, and yet I ache again, and yet I surrender again, to the hunger, to the longing, to the love that ruins me beautifully. You have made me a beggar, a beggar who once had everything, but now has nothing, nothing but longing.

➤ A woman is labelled as insecure and triggered but its more than that. Its hypervigilance. The brain is literally wired to look for signs that's she's unsafe. Her amygdala is an internal fire alarm. Always scanning for signs and feeling alert and on guard all the time. Her man's facial expressions, the ding of his phone, him being distracted, his eyes lingering on someone else. Now that he's hurt her, these all feel like possible signals that he's doing it again. She wants to trust him but she can't.

➤ A promise to stay, to grow, and to choose that person, day after day for a lifetime. To wish to stay with someone until death.

➤ Kiss me in the rain, love me in the dark, hold me till the end and never break my heart.

➤ Even when your heart has been ripped apart and is beyond recognition, even when you've been left alone by the ones you needed most, you still got out of bed to face another day. A brave and strong survivor who makes sure she's a thriver.

➤ She has insecurities, she gets jealous and overthinks everything. She has trust issues, and most days she doesn't think she's good enough. That's who she is and she's not afraid to admit it but you know what? She's amazing in many ways too. She has a huge heart with a lot of scars, a soul that's been through the worst and back. Not everyday is her best, some days she makes mistakes but she learns from them. She's a work in progress and she knows someday she will make someone proud to call her theirs.

➤ Strength to control emotions and not react with anger or defensiveness. Handling situations with patience and wisdom. When a woman is in pain, she needs comfort not conflict. Emotions matter more than just being right in a relationship. Stay calm and speak your hearts out to each other.

➤ A feminine energy deeply craves a space where she can exhale, trust and lean into the masculine's unwavering strength. She yearns to trust his leadership so fully that she can train her mind to release control and flow freely. When the masculine steps into his role with confidence and takes inspired action, the feminine rejoices, feeling safe and cherished. It's in his grounded presence and decisive energy that she finds her freedom to soften, express and thrive.

➤ Sorry is nothing without change. Trust is nothing without proof. Love is nothing without action.

➤ Delaying effort shows your presence isn't a priority. The effort and consistency is what makes a woman feel emotionally safe in what she had in a relationship. The waiting doesn't lead to a step up but it makes the man comfortable.

➤ Emotional security and safety shifts from a cage to a sanctuary of love and connection.

➤ The inability to listen to a woman's words openly and feel into her emotions calmly is a reflection of a man's trauma. When a man is taught that his worth is in his performances and not his feelings, he disowned his emotions a long time ago.

➤ Emotional intimacy simply can't exist without vulnerability.

➤ Loving your partner and them feeling loved are two completely different things. Emotional maturity is realizing that YOU also have toxic traits. It's not always your partner.

➤ Not touching your partner or making eye contact when you're in the same room is a missed opportunity for connection.

➤ What hurt me is that I accepted you for who you were which included lowering my standards, tolerating more than I ever had and standing by you even at the expense of sacrificing my own happiness at times. I tried to convince myself and everyone else that you were worth it. Only to have you prove me wrong and everyone else right. Because what became important to me was finding a way to make US work.

➤ I was okay with being a fool for you if it kept us together. I forgived you even when I knew I couldn't expect any better from you. I became less concerned with being loved the right way and more concerned with making sure I held on to you. I forgot the whole reason I fell for you was in pursuit of happiness, not heartache and hopelessness.

➤ No matter how bad I've been treated, no matter what I've been through or what I'm going through, I still have a genuine heart and endless love to give. That's one thing no one can ever take from me.

➢ Loving you and losing you is the wound that never heals.

➢ One had ego and the other had hope.

➢ You always choose to treat me the way you want to treat me, not the way I want to be treated or the way I deserve to be treated. I used to have so much faith in your love but if your really love me, why do you keep torturing my heart in such a way that I will always feel so unloved and unwanted?

➢ A solution only works if it feels right to both people. If one of you is not comfortable, then it is not a real solution.

➢ The one who has experienced tremendous suffering from those she loved. She might be difficult at times. Her emotions are strong and she won't remain silent. She will challenge you to be better, call you out on your bullshit and carry the weight of the world in her heart. She will love you like nothing you've ever known. If you give her a safe love, she will go to war with you and beside you and face the storm over and over again to protect the one she loves.

➤ She loves with all her heart. Fiercely and without reservations. She'll be the one who stands by you when things fall apart.

➤ She'll cry not because of weakness but because she feels deeply and the emotions are sometimes overwhelming.

➤ Overthinking isn't a flaw, it's how she processes every possibility, every fear, every way to make things better for the both of you.

➤ Healing is a journey not a destination. Find someone willing to learn how to go through it with you. If you can put effort into all other aspects of your life to create a better living then why not put the same effort into your relationship? You make time for what's important to you. Put the same effort into your relationship and see how it becomes amazing.

➤ She'll fight for you, trust you and believe in you and even when she's scared, she'll stand by you. Life with her is a rollercoaster. There will be ups and downs, but the ride is thrilling, unforgettable and full of love.

➤ When a person doesn't know how to accept a version of you, they tend to feel like you are too good for them and push you away. People equate materials to worth and that's why so many feel like if they have nothing, they mean nothing. It's sad.

➤ Some men do not know how to receive that type of woman. Someone who loves them for who they are. Not for what they got.

➤ Effort, consistency and appreciation needs to be reciprocal. If it is not, you will burn yourself out.

➤ A woman wants a man who makes her feel cherished, not pressured. When she trusts that you respect her and she can rely on you emotionally, that's when a real connection forms.

➤ Love is to stand by you not just in moments of joy but in times of struggle, offering support without being asked. Their actions reflect a deep commitment, the kind that isn't driven by obligation but by genuine care.

> ➤ When you fight for someone who goes above and beyond, you nurture a bond built on trust, respect and gratitude. These people are rare. The ones who uplift you when you're down, celebrate your wins like their own and stay when things get difficult. Fighting for them means recognizing their value and showing them the same effort and devotion they give so freely. It's about standing in their corner, making sure they feel seen, appreciated, and supported just as they do for you.

> ➤ True love isn't about being perfect, it's about understanding each other's flaws and working through them together. The struggles we face only makes the bond stronger. When you fight through tough times as a team, you come out even closer on the other side. Learning how your partner wants to be loved is a part of the journey and it makes the relationship even more special. The happiest and strongest couples are the ones who stick together no matter what. In the end, true happiness comes

from overcoming struggles together and appreciating the love that grows through it all.

➤ When you love someone, it is worth fighting for no matter what the odds.

➤ The woman who always puts others first but secretly longs to be chosen was the little girl who felt like she had to earn love.

➤ The woman who craves deep, soul nourishing connections but feels unworthy of them was the little girl who was never truly seen and understood.

➤ Love is not about always getting it right, it is about trying together. You do not have to be completely healed to be deeply loved.

➤ Just because I don't require much doesn't mean I deserve the bare minimum.

➤ We ignore the ones who adore us, adore the ones who ignore us, love the ones who hurt us and hurt the ones that love us.

➤ Being loved is the minimum. Make sure you are also being respected, prioritized, supported, desired and understood.

- Vulnerability is scary but it is the only place where true connection happens.

- Fight, fix and stay. That is maturity. Fighting for love is the hardest everyone fails in. It is about finding the person who will still be standing there wiping the tears away, holding you in their arms after a fight. The one who will never leave no matter how hard things get.

- Love requires emotional endurance. Love does not grow by avoiding pain but by being willing to work through it. It is about staying in the room when the conversation is hard. It is about listening with the intent to understand, not just to reply. It is about doing the uncomfortable work of growth together.

Past Love
(Thank You for the Lessons)

> ➤ Why did you guys break up?

She laughed almost painfully. One day he loved me & the next he didn't.

Strange isn't it? How fast someone's feelings can change & there's nothing you can do but accept it. You have to sit & accept the fact that the person you loved now doesn't even give a shit whether you come or go & frankly that sucks.

> ➤ You who promised me, "I'll always be with you no matter what happens"

> ➤ Like the one before you,

> ➤ You left a deep scar in my heart.

➤ I'm just gonna run right through the rain, I'm just gonna dance through the pain, I'm just gonna feel the rhythm, let my heart beat louder than my head.

➤ There are songs that make you sad when you hear them but it isn't the songs that make you sad. It's the people behind the memories.

➤ She stayed because she loved you but late at night, she's up wondering what that girl had that she doesn't. Now she sees that girl in her mind like a ghost haunting her. You gave her a demon that clings to her shoulders whispering "you're not good enough" over & over again so she's insecure all the time.

➤ I said I was fine but my heart was heavy, my mind was tired and my soul felt lost. I smiled, I carried on and I did what was expected. But deep down, I wished someone would notice, someone who could see beyond the words, hear what I wasn't saying, and understand the weight I was carrying. Because sometimes, "I'm fine" is the easiest way to hide what feels impossible to explain.

➤ They taught us that a man will change for the right woman. Truth is many men miss out on a great woman because they're not mature enough to recognize what a woman brings to the table. A good woman gets hurt because some men don't deal with childhood trauma, past relationships or outgrow the mindset ingrained in them. A man doesn't change for the right woman – he changes when he's ready to become a good man. Don't doubt yourself honey. You have always been the right woman. It was his immaturity that blinded him from seeing everything you gave. So it's not that a man will change for the right woman – it's when he's ready to become the right man. Then he will make the changes.

➤ Another woman will admire the eyes I once loved, but she'll never know the way they once looked at me, with a depth that made me believe I was the centre of his world. Another woman will hold the hands I once held, but she'll never know how their grip felt like home when I was lost. Another woman will call him hers but she'll never know the man I loved, the one who was raw. Another woman will laugh with him and dream with him and maybe even love him but she'll never hold the version of him I once did, the one who was mine in a way he'll never be hers.

➤ You promised me forever but forever was just a moment to you and a lifetime to me. You broke me, piece by piece until I was unrecognizable.

➤ Sometimes I wonder if it was a mistake loving someone so hard and getting so badly hurt in the process. They loved you as if they would never leave you but they left you as if they never loved you.

➤ They met after a long time. He couldn't look into her eyes. After a chaotic silence, he said "I'm sorry." She said "I never wanted you to be mine, I wanted you to make me yours. You broke me so violently that my heart closed all its doors. You can find millions like me but not me anymore, you dropped what was in your hand while trying to pick up from the floor. I wrote you in my every verse that you can't even imagine how I became a poet."

➤ Wild roses grew where you left thorns.

> Grief. The aching void that accumulates over the years. What does it teach us? The ability to be resilient, to strive day after day, even if the void never really fades, we learn to cope in different ways.

> There isn't a single day when I didn't choose you. Even when the world gave me countless reasons to let go, I clung to the fragile hope of us. I stayed when it hurt, loved when it broke me, and fought when I had nothing left to give. I gave you my heart even when yours was elsewhere.

> I hope, in my absence, you finally understand the depth of my love – the love that gave everything even when it received nothing in return. Perhaps my silence will scream the words I never could.

> He fell first. She fell harder. He lost feelings. She can't move on. He broke her heart. She wasn't enough to be his wife but she was enough to meet everyone in his life.

> Whatever I did, I did for love and I have no regrets. I showered you with love and care.

I stepped out of my limits for you. I drained myself just to be with you. I made sure to put you first before anything, even if it meant putting you first before me. I even taught you how to treat me right. I did everything in my part.

➤ You shattered my heart into a million pieces. You made me lose all motivation to do anything. You made me cry harder than ever. You made me lose my appetite. You made me lose track of myself. You destroyed all the progress I made on myself. You made me fall for you when you had no intention of catching me at all. You made me not able to sleep anymore. You gave me nightmares. You broke me. Congratulations.

➤ You weren't the problem. You showed up, poured your heart out and gave your all. Stop letting your wound based guilt deceive you into thinking otherwise. You were enough but they couldn't be enough for you because of their own fears and hurt, and there's nothing you could have ever done to change that.

My Last Lifetime Love & Meri Jaan

(thank you for always inspiring me KUMARESAN GEDIAH):

> Falling for him was not falling at all. It was walking into a house & suddenly knowing you are home.

> It has always been you ever since I first laid my eyes on you. My heart and my mind finally agree on something.

> When you looked into my eyes and said I love you for the first time, I wished for a lifetime of memories with you at that very same moment.

> My soul made love to your soul way before our bodies met. When I first laid eyes on you,

I recognized you. It was like from a different lifetime. You held my heart & my future in your hands.

➤ For it was not into my ear you whispered but into my heart. It was not my lips you kissed but my soul.

➤ What will I pray for him when he is my prayer?

➤ When you're admiring a little too long and realize how beautiful each feature of his face is.

➤ Marry me, let's spend our nights eating cereal on the floor when there is a table behind us. Marry me. We can go to the cinema and sit in the very back row just to make out like kids falling in love for the first time. Marry me, we'll paint the rooms of our house and get more paint on us than on the walls. Marry me. We can hold hands and go to parties that we end up ditching to drink Soju out of the bottle in the bathtub together. Marry me. Slow dance with me in our bedroom with an unmade bed and candles on the nightstand.

➤ I'm his habit, he is my necessity. I'm his demand, he is my life.

➤ Will you still want her after her rage? Do you have the balls to unlock her cage? Careful I tell you, a monster in dead…a viking she seeks, but a wolf she will need. One that will howl at the moon as she does. A wolf that will bite but embrace how she loves.

➤ Nobody talks about the soulmate that walks into your life during your healing era & how hard it is because of both your pain & trauma. We both felt unappreciated & undeserving of love for so long & then all of a sudden we allowed our many walls to come down. We found a best friend & lover in each other. We adore the absolute shit out of each other, the trust & loyalty is unmatched, there's never a dull moment & the love is unconditional. I spent my entire life not knowing this type of love existed & I'm here to tell you, ours does.

➤ The scent of love will always be my weakness and you, you wear it as if it was your natural fragrance.

➤ If I asked you to give me one night under the stars,snuggle beneath the quilts in a truck bed…just to talk…would you ? Just one night to mend the tears, the silence that has been inflicted onto our hearts.

➢ Happiness is waking up in the middle of the night and feeling the heat of the person next to you. You turn around and see them in their most peaceful,innocent and vulnerable state. They breathe as though the weight of the world lays on anyone's shoulder but their own. You smile, kiss their face in the most gentle manner so as not to wake them. You turn around & an involuntary grin forms on your own face. You feel an arm wrap around your waist & you know life doesn't get any better than that moment.

➢ Promise me that you will hug me after a fight. Hold my hand while crossing the road. Cuddle me as we fall asleep. Feed me with your hands. Listen to all my nonsense without getting bored. Hold me tight when I cry. Go on walks with me. Be with me…no matter what comes around.

➢ When I say I love you more, I don't mean I love you more than you love me. Its so much deeper than that. What I mean is that I love you more than the bad days ahead of us both. I love us more than any fight we will ever have. I love you more than the distance that separates you from me. I love you more than any arguments, disagreement or quarrels that we have, big or small. I love you more than all the challenges we both will face together. I love you more than the nights where I'll feel like giving up. I'll love you more than the times you'll end up hurting me. I'll love you more than I'll ever hurt you. I love you more than the greatest adventure I am yet to have, as truly you are the greatest I have ever had. So when I say I love you more, there's so much more behind that than you could ever realize.

➤ When he asked her what he could give her that she'd never had before, she answered "consistency"? If you want to give something no man has ever given me, then don't give me mixed signals nor mixed emotions that leave me wondering. I'm tired of wondering. All I need at this point from someone is consistency.

➤ True love is waking up middle of the night to help you when you're sick because you don't want to be sick alone. Its being your shoulder to cry on, to vent to. True love is being your cheerleader & toughest critic. True love is looking at each other on a spiritual level, a level so deep that you can feel them when they're gone. True love is those little words: " No matter what, I got you always".

➤ I didn't fall in love with you because I was lonely or lost. I fell in love with you because when I saw you for the first time, it was the only time I ever wanted to make someone a permanent part of my world.

➤ Everyone keeps telling me that it'll get better with time, you will find someone else but nobody understands that it's not about finding someone better. I could have a million options in front of me and I would still choose you. I could have all the happiness and easiest life still I would choose to walk with you through all the struggles. I am never going to love someone the way I love you. I will never give your place to anyone because you are my home. I feel like you are my person even if I am not yours. I love you with my heart and soul and it is never going to change.

➢ She stood before him

As you could see into her soul through the light that shone from her eyes

A promise she made within

To always be there for him

No matter what

Through the good and the bad times in life

A promise for this lifetime

➢ She stood before him just as she was made to be, no lies, no judgement & no fake smile. She showed him the storm that raged within her, the strength of her heart & the stubbornness of her will. He saw her every flaw, every doubt, every fear on her face. He saw the spirit & the fire within her & he ran with it.

Despite the storms in life, they set each other ablaze & ran free with the fire that was between them.

Wild, passionate and free.

➢ What's romantic? When he can't hug me tightly & kiss me wildly in public but pulls my cheeks, hold my hand tightly, stares at me, feeds me with his hands, wipes my face with his hanky, plays with my hair, clicks my pictures & treats me like a kid. Trust me, damn romantic.

➢ If a woman is willing to love you when you are broken & when she is broken herself, doesn't leave your side when she sees all your flaws, refuses to give up on you, and is willing to give her all, no matter what. Trust me, she's the one.

➢ Great fucking sex, a good laugh, partner in crime, epic conversations, friendship, honesty, unquestionable loyalty.

➢ I knew I was going to love you before I actually did. There was a pull. There was a strong intuitive feeling that this is it, this is the real deal. This is my person. There was a desire in me to finally put in all the work to heal & be a better me for you & for us. You did things naturally that were suprising to me because no one else had before. My thoughts & feelings were considered. The communication was there. I started settling better boundaries &

standing up for myself more in all areas of my life. Found my divine purpose. Grew closer to God. In falling for you, I fell more in love with myself too.

> Promise me we'll stand by each other through every twist & turn and we'll work together to overcome any obstacles that come our way. I want you to be the one I share my life with & I'll be there for you through all the ups & downs. You aren't just my love, you're also my best friend & I can't imagine my world without you. I love you endlessly.

> If you came to me with a face I have not seen, with a voice I have never heard, I would still know you. Even if centuries separated us, I would still feel you. Somewhere between the sand & the stardust,through every collapse & creation, there is a pulse that echoes of you and I. Love is the only thing we take with us when we leave this world. It is all we carry from one life to the next.

> Falling in love with someone you had no intention of falling for is the most beautiful kind of love. No forcing chemistry or trying to

save them. Just a pure, raw connection created on its own.

➤ This is the kind of love that makes you feel like you could never love this way again. The kind of love where you're lovers and best friends. It's when you can joke around, have unexpected hugs, and random kisses. It's when you two give each other the specific stare and just smile. The kind of love that never ends & enters at just the right time. It's when you can be unapologetically yourself and still be loved. The kind of love that feels once in a lifetime. I think you know what I mean. This is the kind of love that doesn't feel real but it has to be because when our eyes meet, its all I feel.

➤ We're a team. Whatever you lack, I got you. We balance each other out. Minor setback? Guess we'll make a major comeback. Bad day? I promise you a better night. You need support? I'll be your backbone. I'll keep you motivated & at the top always. You got me. I got us.

- Whenever I hug you,I feel my whole universe between my two arms. I feel the protection within that no one can harm. My heart starts racing with yours,relaxing it's every cores. Every beat of our hearts shares perfect sync, I couldn't write to you how it feels, the way I think. My mind suddenly stops reacting to anything else, except the relief that every burden of my heart melts. I feel my heart leaping from my chest to yours, whenever I hold you close, the world is ours. My soul travels from the stars to the ground, I feel like I'm lost and yet found.

- "I'm at my worst" he murmured. She held his hand gently and replied, "Don't worry, we'll face this together. Soon, you'll come out of this – I promise". He sighed and said "I don't know where life is taking me". With a soft smile, she looked into his eyes and said "Wherever it leads, I'll be right there, following you every step of the way".

- It made me realize that perhaps he became too comfortable, so ease in our relationship that he's forgotten to nurture the things that make me feel loved and valued. Instead of understanding my emotions, he's quick to label me as difficult. All I really want is for him to show me I'm still a priority.

➤ She noticed it all. The slower response times. The loss of energy that was once there. The lack of quality time and communication. The missing sparkle from the reflection in your eyes as you made eye contact. She noticed it all but held on longer because she loved you.

➤ She's been different. You can see it in the way she's stopped trying to hide the bags under her eyes, the way she lets the clothes hang loose instead of forcing a smile into something "cute". Her world's falling apart but she's pretending it's not. Check on her. She needs someone to remind her it's okay to fall apart, that it's okay to not always be fine. She's not okay. She needs you.

➤ You'll never taste the promises we made in silence or feel the fire that only we could ignite in one single touch. You'll never know how your hands wiped away my tears as they were your own. You'll never hear the heartbeat that raced when we are close or know the comfort of falling asleep to its rhythm like a song meant only for me. You'll never know how much I miss the man who was vulnerable, the one who gave me his mornings and nights. You'll never know the love that once consumed us, a love that imperfect, messy but undeniably ours.

➢ I knew you would be the one to hurt me. I knew it from the moment we met but I still didn't care. I know it would happen all along and I've just been waiting, just collecting piece after piece trying to put myself back together again because I don't recognize myself anymore.

➢ You breathed life back into my heart when I thought it had forgotten how to beat. Every time our eyes meet, it's like the whole world fades away. I see our future unfolding, the lazy mornings, the adventures we'll share, the quiet moments that'll mean everything. I want it all with you. The silly arguments over what movie to watch. The comfort of your arms when life gets tough. You're not just another chapter in my story. You're the ink to my pen, the pages of my book. You're the reason I wake up with a smile, the last thought before I drift off to sleep. So please, never doubt your place in my life. You're not just someone. You're my someone. In a life full of noise, you're my favourite song. You're the love I didn't know I was waiting for and now that I've found you, I'm never letting you go.

➤ Because you're it for me. Whether it's today, tomorrow, a year or decades from now, that'll never change.

➤ Taking breaks or space doesn't solve problems. Listening, compromise and teamwork do.

➤ The push-pull dynamic is the issue not our partner. We're teammates against the dynamic.

➤ Take me back to those happy days when you cared for me in so many ways, when every look and every touch showed me that I meant so much. Take me back to that special time when every moment felt so right and dreams of us filled every night.

➢ She wants a soft connection. She wants to be asked about her day and is she is okay. She wants forehead kisses. She wants the back of her hand kissed at red lights. She wants to hold hands and be lead into a crowd. She wants romantic gestures. She wants her hair played with until she falls asleep. She wants the kind of relationship that makes people stop and say "You can tell they really love each other".

➢ The more time I spend with you, the less time I spend in my head. The more I talk to you, the less I listen to my demons. The more I share with you, the less I feel the need to hide. The more I love you, the less I need anything else.

➢ She was the "Man" of her family. He was the only son. He took care of her sad inner child and she turned his loneliness in laughter. He gave her everything she never once asked for, she let herself fall in his arms when the world scared her. He created a space where she was free and for the first time, she embraced being a woman.

➢ I fell in love with a person whose darkness I recognized as I did my own. My monsters found a home in you. That's the kind of love that owns your skin and bones. Love is found in the darkness because it is the candle in the night.

➤ When I met him and fell into his arms, I could've slept for a thousand years. I was safe. I didn't know how to trust there was no reason to run and the chaos was over. My skin would itch. I didn't understand how someone could love me. I didn't know how to accept more when I fully believed I deserved less.

➤ She got so attached to you because you were the reason she wished the days would go by faster just to see you again, you were the first person she never wanted to stop talking to and you were the first person she wanted romantically after spending so long alone.

➤ Forgetting you is impossible, not because my memory won't allow it but because you've written yourself into the story of my soul.

➤ What if he took my whole heart & gave it back into pieces, pieces I could never mend? What if he got so close to me only to drift far away? What if he took all of me & left me utterly alone? What if he was just for the days, not for a lifetime? What if his promises were whispers carried by the wind? What if my soul becomes a poem he reads once & forgets? And in that silence, her heart whispered…What if he loved you so deeply, he could heal every scar you carry? What if he loved you because you were all he ever wanted? What if you are the most beautiful part of his life, the piece he never knew was missing? What if he is me? What if I will keep you as my forever, holding your heart as carefully as my own?

➢ I used to think I wanted the perfect romance with the fairy tale ending but with you, I want everything. I want to be with you on your worst days, I want to take care of you when you're sick, I want to lift you up when you're down, I want to support you through every struggle, I want to hold your hand through every storm, and I want your love in all its messy, agonizing and exhilarating glory. Because I realize now that true love isn't always pretty, but it is always beautiful. As long as I'm with you.

- ➤ I promise to always hold space for you even when the world feels heavy. To listen not just to your words but to the emotions behind them. I promise to be your safe place where you can lay down your burdens and simply be yourself. I vow to never take your love for granted to celebrate the small quiet moments just as much as the big ones. To choose you every day, even when it's hard, and to work through the storms instead of running from them. I promise to remind you with every action how deeply you're cherished. To grow with you, to laugh with you and love you in ways that make you feel seen, valued and endlessly appreciated. You have my heart & I promise to hold yours with the utmost care.

- ➤ You must take a chance. If you wait for the perfect weather, you'll never plant your seeds. If you're afraid that every cloud will bring rain, you will never harvest your crops. You don't know where the wind blows. And you don't know how a baby grows in its mother's womb. In the same way, you never know till you take a leap of faith and make it happen.

- She wants romance. She wants intimacy. She wants to be able to look her man into his eyes and only see his true love for her just as she has for him. She wants date nights. She wants loyalty. She wants to be able to come home after a long day and feel nothing but love. She wants it because she can return it.

- Reassurance. Intimacy. Little reminders. It doesn't have to be big things. It can be a kiss on the forehead, a little note left around the house. You don't have to pour your heart out all the time. Just show me in little ways that I'm yours.

- The way she loved was different. Like something no one has ever seen before. Deep. Selfless. Intense. It was the kind of love people spend their whole lives searching for and some don't even recognize it. She gave without expecting anything in return, pouring into someone even when her own cup was empty. Her love terrified him. It was too real, too raw.

- When everyone was asleep and the world was quiet, her eyes flooded with the memories of him. She could see his smile, hear his voice, feel his touch. It was replaying a movie she knew by heart but couldn't bear to watch without him.

➤ An intimate relationship is also an opportunity for both to heal the wounds of the past and grow stronger apart from lighting the fires of passion. The deepest work is done in partnership, with two heart connected individuals seeing the issues that trigger each other as a gift, or a clue, to their healing rather than an obstacle. And two people can help each other to heal can also help each other to love more.

➤ You're woven into who I am, stitched into my soul. You're there in every broken piece. You're my heartbeat, the one thing that keeps me from giving up, the one thing that makes me feel that love can be real, even when it hurts. You're the fire inside me, even when it burns and even when its feels too much to bear. I would rather live with this love, even if it consumes me than live without it. I can't forget you because you're a part of me.

➢ You're the pulse within my heart, the thread holding my shattered soul together, the gravity that keeps me from unraveling. You're not a piece of my story, you're the ink that writes it, the pages that cradle my existence. Each kiss a vow, each touch a promise. You don't see me but I'm there, watching, yearning & aching. You can't hear my heart but it beats for you alone. Every pulse is a cry: Let me love you, let me belong to you. Even as my love burns in the shadows, I am yours. I love you with a fire so fierce it could set the stars ablaze. Even when the universe crumbles, I will search for you in the ashes that once was and I will love you still, Now. Always. Forever.

➢ You're not just my desire. You're my solace, my torment, my sanctuary, my storm. You're the fire that scorches my nights. The dream that haunts me day and night. You're buried too deep inside me, in the marrow of my bones, in the quiet of my soul. You're carved into my soul, in every heartbeat and every breath. A love that burns but never dies. Stay. Stay and see the mess that I am, feel the love that bleeds through every broken part of me.

I'll give you everything what's shattered and what's still whole if you'll just let me show you the depth of what I feel.

➤ Real love shows up when you're at your lowest, when everything feels like it's falling apart, love is when they sit with you in silence when you have no words, listen to your fears without rushing to fix them. It's holding you when you're anxious, comforting you when you're struggling, staying by your side through the chaos. Love isn't grand gestures, it's in the everyday actions that remind you that you matter. When their actions match their words, you'll feel it.

➤ To be loved right, loved fully, without measure, and without hesitation. To be prioritized, adored, and wholesomely cared for. To be love with zero fear of the future or past, with no doubt in my heart, only faith in my love and in the one I've chosen to share it with.

➤ You hit roadblocks together & decide how to get past them as a team. You discover that you're not aligned in some areas & you work towards meeting in the middle. You become fluent in each other. And the work never ends. Becoming the one for the person you want to do life with is how you stay the one.

➤ You're my love, my headache, my smile, my frown, my right, my wrong, my happiness, my pain and my everything.

➤ You're mine but you are not mine. I am yours but you hardly know it.

➤ You have everything you need, only when you love what you have.

➤ My heart only ever had one thought, one want. One need. Despite all, in spite of all, all my heart has ever wanted is you.

➤ I miss how you wanted me, I miss you, the old you, the one who used to love me and make me feel like there was just you & me.

➤ Its just hard to think I'll never get the chance to say you're mine

➤ There are moments in my life that I will always remember not because they were important, but because you were there.

- Choose to love each other even in those moments when you struggle to like each other. Love is a commitment not a feeling.

- I want all of it. I want the pointless bickering, the long walks, the late night phone calls, the good morning texts. I want photos with you, to hold your hand, to call you Jaan. The joking, the wrestling, the fights. I want to be the inseparable best friend couple that people are like "you're still together"? That's what I want. I want you. I want us.

- A man that stares at you like you're the prettiest demon he's ever seen in his life.

- My goal is to marry you and grow with you. I'm not dating to waste time because I see everything in you and in us.

- A marriage. Not just a wedding. A family. Not just a baby. A home. Not just a house. A future. Not just promises.

- I don't want to settle for a lazy relationship. I want to be appreciated. I want to feel special every day, not just sometimes. I want effort, care and love. I want to know I matter, not feel like an afterthought. I want love that shows in actions, not just words. I want a bond that stays strong, not one that fades over. I love the random stories and mentions. I want the thoughtful texts, the surprise hugs, and the little moments that show I'm on your mind. I want the late night talks, the laughter over silly things, and the comfort of knowing I'm safe with you. I want effort, love, and a connection that feels real every single day.

➤ The intimacy of being tired together. A head on a chest while falling asleep to the thump.. thump..thump.. of your love's heart. Those delirius giggles you get directed at nothing in particular. To be wrapped in a coccon of blankets on a cold winter's night, bodies as close & as intertwined as humanly possible to keep warm. There's nothing more I want than to drift off in the arms of the one I love.

➤ Intimacy is safety. Safety in the embrace of the one you love, warmth of one soul in two bodies, instant connection, eye to eye contact, skin to skin, BARE GENUINE AND RAW.

➤ That kinda love where you won't get me flowers everyday but figure out something's off by the slightest change in my tone. A love where you understand that a forehead kiss means a lot but a kiss on the lips sends my heart into a frenzy everytime. A love where we talk about every problem we face. A love where we tell each other stuff. A love where we grow together. A love a little bit different. A love not everyone can have. A love we're lucky to have.

➤ Don't get me wrong, call me a passionate lover. I have your name written on the walls of my heart. My heart, my beloved, my love's desire…may you not burn from the passion of my love.

➤ Love is giving someone the chance to destroy you down till your soul & trusting that they won't. In other words, blind faith.

➤ A journey of a lifetime, woven across time, intertwined souls, under the stars and under the skies. Like the moon, different phases, not fully whole but beautiful just the same. A serene light that shines the way through the tunnel of darkness.

➤ Ignited desire, flamed by the embers of a spark. Throbbing at every pulse.

➤ A great partner will still bring out your triggers, wounds from the past, fears, insecurities and limiting beliefs. A secure healthy partnership will provide you with a safe space to work through those things and become a better version of yourself.

➤ If we've come this close to losing each other but still can't imagine life apart, maybe it's time to let go of our pride and build the kind of life we've always dreamed of – one that brings us security and peace. Let's support each other and grow together so we never have to face that edge again.

➤ You know she's real when you & her are unofficial and she's still there for you. You know she's real when you're unsure how you feel about her & she's still waiting for you. You know she's real when she trusts you even after you're hurt her multiple times with your words and actions. You know she's real when you would hurt her & she's still caring about you as if it never happened. Don't lose a special girl like that because that's what its like when someone is meant for you.

➢ Someone who will choose to stay. Someone who feels like home and someone who also finds home in me.

➢ If you love an overthinker, there are things you need to know. Their neediness isn't simply neediness – its fear. I promise you, no one is more tired by their overactive mind than they are. They live with it every day, and wish they could live life without the dozen hypotheticals invading each moment. But they can't. It's sometimes difficult to see, but there is beauty in over thinking. Those people who are most afraid to hurt are also the ones who love the most. If you love an overthinker, you should appreciate that. Be there for them. Tell them you're not going away. Reassure them. They are still learning to trust. They're learning to let go of their fears because the one before you walked away after love got a little hard.

They are fighting every day to win the biggest battle, the battle against their own mind.

➢ Love isn't just in the easy days, in the sunshine, in the laughter, in the warmth. Love is in the trenches, too. It's in the slammed doors, the quiet nights filled with distance, the "I don't know how to fix this" moments. It's in the choice to stay when leaving would be easier. In the reaching, the forgiving, the deep breath before saying "Let's try again". Because real love? It doesn't quit when it gets hard. It digs in, it holds on, and it refuses to let go.

➢ Everyone talks about falling in love, but no one talks about staying in love. It's the little things – the effort, the patience, the choice to show up even when it's tough. Love isn't just about the initial spark, it's about keeping the fire alive even on the tough days.

➢ It's not like we visually see other men as unattractive because yes there are beautiful people in this world, but it's like their attractiveness becomes plain. We think "Yeah just another attractive man but he's not my man" just another basic good looking guy. It's not a turn on to see them, only your man can make you feel more.

➤ All that I have is yours. The late night conversations, the messy mornings, every half finished thought and the silence in between. Take my bad days, the missed calls, the nervous smiles, the way I overthink everything and the still find peace with you. Every detail, even the ones I'm afraid to show, they belong to you now. I give you my awkward pauses, my stumbling words, the dreams I haven't spoken yet. I give you the parts of me I'm still figuring out, the way my heart beats differently when you're near, the way the world feels smaller but somehow enough. There's nothing I hold back – no second thoughts, no hidden corners. Everything that I am, imperfect, unfinished, is YOURS.

➤ You asked for space and I gave it to you. You said that it's not about me. That you needed a little time for yourself. And I wanted to be understanding. I didn't want to be the kind of person who panics when things start to shift a little. So, I loosened my grip. Gave you the space to breathe. To think. To stretch into whoever you were trying to become. At first, it felt right. Healthy, even. We still talked, still laughed, still carried pieces of each other in our pockets. You were still there, just a little less. A little more distant in ways that were too subtle to call out but too sharp to ignore. I told myself it was okay. That you just needed time. That space didn't have to mean distance. That distance didn't have to mean I was losing you. But the thing about space is that if you give someone too much of it, they start to forget how to come back. And that's what happened isn't it? You still let me in but only in parts of your life that didn't require too much of you. And I get it. People change. But you didn't just grow. You outgrew me. Distanced yourself in ways I couldn't keep up with. I only wanted to give you space. Never to lose you. I really thought that when you were done finding yourself, you'd still want to find me, too.

> He gazes down at her as she sleeps, her face nestled against his chest, her breath soft and steady. "Be mine forever," he whispers, his voice barely audible in the quiet room. "I can't

bear the thought of you belonging to anyone else. It would break my heart, princess." She moves slightly, mumbling something incoherent in her sleep, drawing a faint smile to his lips. "That's my good girl," he murmurs, pressing a gentle kiss to her hair. "I love you more than anything. You're my everything, sweetheart."

➤ Making love while the sun rises slowly, you're both half unconscious and in need of each other's skin and then sleeping right after is both beautiful and deadening.

➤ The feeling when it's early morning & he's kissing your skin through your clothes. His hands are wandering & shaking. You're both half asleep but you're feeling the fiery sensation in your veins, on your skin as he's dragging your clothes off of you. And you both can't help it.

➤ You ask him "are you hungry?" He says "you have no idea." Then he snatches your waist & sets you on the dinner table, staring into your surprised eyes with a darkened gaze unbuckling his belt in between your legs.

> When he's a dominant masculine man, but only you can make him helpless. He loves it when you kneel, with him in your mouth, your eyes holding frustration, his throat vibrating with emotions, his sounds becoming more uncontrolled. His hands reach for you, wanting you to stop, to kiss you, to be inside you, and to maybe show you at least half of what you mean to him. He's a dominant masculine man but the things only you can do to him, even in the simplest ways are beyond his grasp.

> "I don't know." She whispers. "I don't know how I can make you happy?" she asks. "Teach me." He looks at her, his heart filling with many emotions. Someone really made him feel that his happiness matters too. "Make me yours then." He sighs, gently holding her hands in his. "Because you already make me happy. Let me makes us happy. Together." She cups his face in her hands, smiling wide. "Darling, you are already mine." "Yes." His lips brush against her forehead. "I am yours." To be hers is one of the biggest happiness of his life. He belongs to her.

- ➤ "What do you want?" she asked exasperatedly as she lifted her tired eyes to meet his concerned ones. He moved closer until he was standing right before her, "I want to know why you've been avoiding me recently."

- ➤ "I wasn't avoiding you," she sighed but he cut her off, "Don't lie to me." She tensed slightly as she fumbled with the words in her head. He tipped her chin up with his hand, "Talk to me,darling."

- ➤ "I'm avoiding you because there's a possibility that I may deeply fall in love with you and I won't be able to go back if I did," she whispered softly as her heart clenched. He blew out a rough breath as he pressed her forehead against his, "Is that such a bad thing?"

- ➤ She brought her hands up to his chest, fisting his shirt in her hands, "It is. I wouldn't do that to you." He sighed softly before cupping her face with his hands, "But what if I so deeply wanted to be loved by you? I've seen how it is when you love something and I can't help but wish to be loved the same way. To be loved through my darkness and flaws. To be loved so endearingly that preserves my existence on the pages that were kissed by your fingertips. And the most beautiful of all, to be loved by you."

➤ She chose you over everyone else and you chose everyone else over her

➤ In another life, I hope I can be loved without begging and without having to worry about anything. In another life, I hope I don't have to explain how I want to be loved. Or have to beg how to be treated right. In another life, I hope I'm enough.

➤ I didn't fall in love with you. I chose to be in love with you. I knew all odds were against us yet I didn't think twice before loving you. Your presence, the warmth of your skin against mine, the look in your eyes, the comfort in your hugs, the way your lips brushed against mine, the long drives and endless laughter, the walks and the 2am adventures, the urge to see each other again after spending the entire night together, yet these aren't the reasons for why I love you. It's the kind of love where I knew I was setting myself up for a tragedy but I held on to you still, knowing you'd never feel the same but I gave in anyway. I'd still hold on to you for as long as you'd want me to even if it meant hurting myself because my love for you was always unconditional baby and I'd do it over and over again.

➤ True love isn't about perfect moments. It's about the imperfect ones we navigate together. Its not just holding hands on sunny days but standing side by side in the storms. With you, I've learned that love is about patience, forgiveness, and choosing each other every single day. You're my calm in the chaos, my laughter in the silence and my reason to believe in forever. With every step we take, we're writing a story of trust, devotion and endless possibilities. You're my greatest adventure, my safe place, and my everything. Here's to us, now and always.

➤ Honestly, I can't wait for the days I get to run around the house with you. The nights I get to roll over & see you peacefully sleeping. The evenings I get to take you to dinner. The nights where we stay in & watch stupid movies all night. The days we go on random adventures with no destination. Midnight trips to the store because we were hungry & ran out of alcohol. The mornings I get to cook you breakfast. I just can't wait to experience life with you for a lifetime which is why I want it to start as fast as it can.

➤ Domestic sweetness. Cooking dinner with the one you love while they wrap their arms around you. Taking quick kiss breaks in between folding fresh laundry. Washing each other's hair in the shower. Giggling & rolling around in fresh sheets you both just finished putting on. Dusting while showing off your latest dance moves & having your sweetheart show off their vocals. It's so comforting to have someone that you just enjoy making a home with. Because chores done with someone you love isn't such a chore after all.

➤ She was the girl who was always done wrong but she didn't want you to feel that so she was always trying to make you happy. She was the girl who tried even though you kept a barrier distance but she stayed and this girl loves you so much more than her own self.

➤ I listen to you with my eyes, feel you with my lips, talk to you with my hands, and taste you with my soul. My skin remembers you & my mind shivers to your touch. I love you in ways no other ever will.

➤ She's not like the women you're used to. She won't cheat on you, won't try to control you, and won't play games. All she wants is to be with you – even if its just a quick trip to the gas station – she'll jump at any chance to spend time together. She'll check in on you, make sure you're okay and surprise you with your favourite meal or drink just because she cares. She'll be your rock, your peace, the person you can always count on. She doesn't care about how much money you have or what car you drive. She just wants you - your time, your presence, your love. She's the kind of woman who values the little things, which sees the real you and all she asks is that you see her too.

➤ It's the strength in how he holds my hand when I'm worried. How his fingers intertwine with mine like an anchor in the storm. It's the way he steadies my breath without saying a word, how his presence alone makes the world feel a little less heavy. It's the comfort of sitting in silence without needing to fill it, how he looks at me and truly sees me, the messy, imperfect, beautiful me. It's the way he knows I'm not okay without me saying anything, how he reads the heaviness in my silence, the truth behind my "I'm fine." It's in the soft squeeze of reassurance, the gentle rub of his thumb against my skin as if to say "I'm here, we'll get through this." It's the calmness in his eyes when mine are filled with fear, how he grounds me when my mind is spinning. It's not about the proximity of our bodies, it's about the closeness of our souls, it's the rush of passion, it's not just the way he traces my skin but in the way he traces my scars with fingers soft enough to make the broken pieces feel beautiful.

➤ When I said I love you, I wasn't just offering words; I was surrendering my soul. I didn't mean I want you in passing desire; I meant I need you like the earth needs the sun, like lungs crave air. When I said I love you, I meant you are my belonging, my safe place, my home. I wanted to pour myself into you, to learn your every thought, to trace the unspoken words in your silence. I would give up every fragment of myself just to complete you, to be the missing piece you never knew you needed.

➤ There is beauty in loving someone even if they don't love you back the same way and for that I regret nothing.

➤ You know she's real when you're unsure about how you feel about her and she's still waiting for you. You know she's real when you tend to push her away and she still keeps coming back. You know she's real when you would hurt her and she still cares about you as if it never happened. That's what it's like when someone is meant for you.

➤ I let you in. Not just into my life, but into the deepest parts of me, the places I kept hidden from the world. I showed you my scars, the ones that still ached on the darkest of nights.

➤ Coming together with someone is meant to make your life more beautiful, more easeful, more supported, just lighter. You are not meant to be at war, finding faults and irritations and competing with each other about who knows better. You are both completely different, unique human beings, both with strengths and weaknesses. You are meant to have things about you that your partner doesn't, that is why it is a mirror reflection – to show each other exactly where to grow. Unfortunately, too often, we do not want to face the growth so we attack the person who is actually there for our expansion. You need to care, you need to listen, you need to learn about each other, you need to hear how you both feel loved, what you both need. You also need to hear their perceptions, opinions, insights and feelings even when they are uncomfortable and especially when you do not understand. Your ego needs to stop getting in the way. Be best friends, lovers, laugh, enjoy each other's company, draw on each other's strengths, support each other in the places that need support, learn how to repair and say sorry and make all decisions from a place of kindness and love. Work with each other, not against each other. The fighting, the disagreements, the combat between egos is not necessary, it is just relationship sabotage. Remember how much you loved them in the beginning. Stop taking it for granted.

➤ I want you. I want to hear from you that you miss me, even when I'm not around. I want random updates even about the smallest things. I want you to hold my hand like you mean it, like I matter. I want you to call me at unexpected times just to say you miss me. I want to be loved not just with words, not just with things, but with presence, with effort, with heart. That's all I want.

➤ You came into my life at an unexpected time and I found myself slowly wanting to create a lifetime of memories with you.

➤ Behind this girl is a girl who will never lose her love for you. A girl who fights daily to keep you in her life. She tries to work things out even though it may seem too far gone. If you love her like you say you do then fight for her just like how she fights for you. Don't let one or a couple of bad days change how you feel for her. Because there would be no other girl like her that would give you her world even when she's falling apart.

➤ A best friend I make love to, hustle with, travel with, shop with, club with and live with. A partner in crime, a life partner. I trust you with my heart.

➤ Long hugs, kisses on the neck, cuddling, passionate slow kissing, watching you sleep and protecting you, staring deep into your eyes and seeing your soul while stroking your hair and kissing your lips.

➤ Let my soul be your soul and let your soul be my soul.

➤ I want to talk to you and hear about your day. I want to listen to your heart while I lay on your chest. I want to interlock hands, kiss your lips and whisper into your ear to tell you that I've got you, always. I want you to know that I won't leave you during this lifetime or the next because I intend for our souls to never part ways.

> ➤ I let you see me naked. Truly naked; mentally, emotionally and spiritually. I bared myself to you. I let your hands race over wounds that I hid before. I trusted you and we sat as I told you the stories of people you would never wish to meet but I did. Of experiences I would never wish upon you, but I survived. I let you see beneath the sheet of the person that I let others see and you stayed. Unmoved by what I thought would make you leave. You bundled me in your arms and I felt unknown wounds fade. In that moment, I knew, this love would never leave me the same. Loving you was always a beautiful change.

> ➤ I knew from the beginning that smile would be the end of me. The way you look at me, touch me, kiss me. It won't always be easy, I know that. But trust me, I won't leave. If you're staying, I'm staying.

> ➤ I'd cut my soul into a million different pieces just to form a constellation to light your way home. I'd write love poems to the parts of yourself you can't stand. I'd stand in the shadows of your heart and tell you I'm not afraid of your dark.

- Your voice isn't just any voice, its special. It's the calm that washes over me like a warm summer rain, it's the light that scatters the darkness like a sunrise, it's the once numb heart that feels so deeply again.

- The thought of you, the smell of you, the essence of being with you never left my mind. A million things may come and go but the core of my being holds onto the memories that we ever made – the good, the bad and the crispy, everything intertwined.

- A woman will put aside her happiness for her man but a man will put his woman aside for his happiness. Sounds harsh but it is true.

- Taking breaks or space do not solve problems. Listening, compromise and teamwork does.

- Protecting her heart is a daily commitment, not just in grand gestures but in the small choices you make, like choosing to keep your challenges private. It's about recognizing the power of your words and how they can either build or break the foundation of your love. Love her in a way that makes her feel cherished every day.

- I'm not leaving over an argument. I'm not leaving because you have unhealed wounds, I'm not leaving because you sometimes say the wrong things. The reason I'm not leaving is because nobody showed you how to properly communicate. We will learn together. We will grow together.

- Even though I called you mine, I was never really yours.

- I think the problem is that I'm so deeply in love with him that I would let him drag me to hell if it meant I get to hold his hand on the way down.

- It is your imprint that remains on my heart.

- The walls of her heart were decorated with nightmares and yet she believed in fairytales.

- The push-pull dynamic is the issue not our partner. We are teammates against the dynamic.

- I promise to always take your pain seriously. If it hurts you, it matters to me.

> The day I finally saw you, my soul spoke to me. This is it. This is your home.

> Hug me tight and then tighter. Let this soul dissolve in you, do not let me go until I smell like you.

> There may be storms and challenges along the way but I am committed to working through them with him. He has hurt me but I also know he has the power to heal me. He is the one who fills the void in my heart and I choose to love him with all of my being, in the calm and sweet moments as well as the difficult ones.

> When I wrap my arms around you, I'm pouring out my feelings without words. I wish I could keep hugging you forever, never letting go because in those moments, each time our embrace lingers, I find myself silently asking, could this moment stretch into eternity? A profound connection and an unspoken language of affection where feelings transcends speech. In your embrace, time stands still and all that matters is the warmth and love we share. It's a hug that

speaks volumes, a testament to the depth of my emotions for you.

➤ If it were up to me, I'd marry you right now. I'd start my life with you. We'd build a cute little house. Make love, cuddle by the fireplace and eat breakfast together the next morning. Get into bad fights but make up just as quick. Small suprises time to time from each other, watch the sunset every evening from our balcony. Watch our babies grow up. Hold each other every night and never forget the love that started this all. If it were up to me, I'd start that adventure with you right now.

➤ Take a chance on me. I know those words are wrought with uncertainty. I know the chances you've taken before have left you high and dry. I know you're scared after everything before this has failed you and so am I but baby, if I have to fail again, it is you I want to go down in flames with. If it does work out, it would be this. It would be you and me and this fire between us. Take a chance on me because the timing is always going to be wrong and the stars are never going to align but we could cast all that aside and give in. Give in to the complete impossibility that this could work despite everything that stands in our way. Give in to that this will be worth it in the end. Give in to senselessness. Give in to you, finally giving in to me.

➢ Being able to wake up next to you in the mornings, have a fresh cup of coffee and watch the sunrise together. Thank you for being my beacon. I can't wait until it's just us two living together and never having to say goodbye. I honestly can't wait to see what the world has in store for us.

➢ Some part of me will always be stuck on you. Maybe because you are the first person I've truly unconditionally loved. No matter the reason, I could never stop loving you.

➢ I am infinitely yours. Every day for all the days. In this life and in every life, I choose you.